No Lex 10-12

A MAN NAMED THOREAU
by Robert Burleigh

illustrated by Lloyd Bloom

Atheneum   New York

Library of Congress Cataloging in Publication Data

Burleigh, Robert.
A man named Thoreau.

SUMMARY: Presents the life and ideas of the renowned
nineteenth-century American author.
1. Thoreau, Henry David, 1817–1862—Biography—
Juvenile literature. 2. Authors, American—19th century—
Biography—Juvenile literature. [1. Thoreau, Henry David,
1817–1862. 2. Authors, American] I. Bloom, Lloyd, ill.
II. Title.
PS3053.B79   1985   818'.309 [B] [92]   85-7947
ISBN 0-689-31122-2

Atheneum
Macmillan Publishing Company
866 Third Avenue, New York, NY 10022
Collier Macmillan Canada, Inc.

Typography by Mary Ahern

5 7 9 11 13 15 17 19   20 18 16 14 12 10 8 6 4

If you have built castles in the air, your work
need not be lost; that is where they should be.
Now put the foundations under them.

from WALDEN

HIS NAME WAS THOREAU. Henry David Thoreau. He lived in America over one hundred years ago, in the small village of Concord, Massachusetts.

All the people in Concord knew Thoreau, for his family had lived there since he was a small boy. Many of them thought he was a bit strange. Every day, clear or cloudy, summer or winter, the young man Thoreau would take long walks in the woods and fields around the town. "There goes Thoreau," some said. While others, knowing that he was a recent graduate of Harvard College, asked impatiently, "Why doesn't he *do* something? He's always just walking around!"

But Thoreau *was* doing something. He was thinking. And he was observing the animals and rivers and trees. He wanted to see and feel as much as he could. Then, each night, he wrote down what he had seen that day, along with the thoughts he had.

Above all, Thoreau wanted to live his own kind of life. He believed that a person might live differently from his neighbors because he heard a "different drummer." If so, "let him step to the music which he hears," Thoreau wrote, "however measured or far away."

There was a small lake, or pond, near Concord, named Walden. Thoreau especially liked to walk in the woods beside it. Often he would sit by the water and listen to its soft ripples. He loved Walden's bluey-green stillness. "A lake is like an eye of the earth," he once said.

One spring, when Thoreau was in his late twenties, he decided to build a little house, or hut, on one of Walden's shores. It was not far from Concord, but it was a place where he could be alone. The house he built was very simple. It had one room, one table, a bed, and three chairs. Thoreau later counted up what the house and the furniture cost, down to the very last penny. And everything came to just $28.12½.

Now more than ever before he could spend his time as he wished. In warm weather, he started each day by taking a swim. Then he hoed a bean field he had planted. Someone asked him why he—a writer and a thinker—was spending his time in a field. "I want to make the earth say 'Beans' instead of 'Grass,'" he answered with a smile.

After hoeing, he read a little, or wrote at his small desk. Then he swam once more and went walking, sometimes in the woods, sometimes to the town. At other times, however, he went nowhere and did nothing. The day seemed too fine to do more than just sit quietly and look and listen. But Thoreau didn't think this time was wasted either. "In seasons like those," he remembered later, "I grew like corn in the night."

But what was Thoreau really searching for? He felt there was something wild and fresh in nature. He wasn't sure what it was, but he knew it was there. In winter, he would kneel on the cold, clear ice and stare down "into the quiet parlor of the fishes." One fish he saw is called a pickerel. He would watch the pickerel come and go for a long time. For it seemed to him that this beautiful, slow-moving creature had been formed from the pure Walden water itself!

Another time, he held a baby partridge in the palm of his hand and looked into its eyes. The tiny bird didn't move, but only stared back. Such a gaze, Thoreau thought, was not born when the bird was. No, it was so calm and clear that it must have been created long, long ago—with the sky!

To Thoreau, nature was like a living being. He wanted to do more than just enjoy its beauty. He wanted to get so close to nature that he became one with it. Others went fishing in Walden for fish; Thoreau felt he was "angling for the pond itself." Others went fox hunting; Thoreau once jogged for miles through deep snow, following a fox until he actually ran it down (and let it go). Others, if they had discovered (as Thoreau did) a new kind of fish, would weigh it or eat it; but Thoreau just wanted to "think for a moment like a bream [that fish]."

He was always finding small, out-of-the-way things to excite him, or call forth a memorable phrase. One whole morning he lay on his stomach and watched a war between red and black ants. Once a mouse ran up his sleeve as he sat outside eating. When Thoreau fed the tiny creature some cheese, he watched it nibble and then clean its face with its paws "like a fly." The first birds of spring sounded to him like "the last snowflakes of winter tinkling as they fell." On certain days, he heard the ring of church bells, carried on the wind from nearby towns. As the bell-sounds echoed softly above him, Thoreau imagined the wind was playing through the pines like fingers moving over green harp strings.

But Thoreau had another important reason for going to live at Walden. He wanted to prove something to himself—and to other people, too. He wanted to show that someone could live very, very simply. The great mass of people, he was sure, were not happy. They lived lives of "quiet desperation." They seemed to Thoreau to work hard to own things, which, when they finally got them, left them still unsatisfied. The things became, we might say, more trouble in getting and keeping than they were worth. "It's easier to *get* a house than to get rid of it," Thoreau wrote. Another time he said: "It's never clear if the man owns the house—or the house owns the man."

Indeed, Thoreau had an unusual way of estimating something's true value. He did not count what it cost in dollars and cents. Instead, he counted what it cost in terms of "the amount of what I call life that must be exchanged for it." Did a house cost (in those far-off times) five thousand dollars? Thoreau would say no—its real cost is the many years of (perhaps unpleasant) labor one must spend to get the money to buy the house!

That's why Thoreau's house was simple and his food was plain. Getting these necessary things took him little time. And this left him free, he felt, to do what he really wanted to do: to see and learn and, most of all, think and write. "My greatest skill," he once said, "has been to want but little," a trait which he sometimes took to humorous extremes. He tells us that he once had three large and beautiful stones on his desk. "I found, however," he writes, "that I had to dust them each day—while the furniture of my mind was still undusted." So he threw the stones out!

"Simplicity, simplicity, simplicity!" Such was his motto. Wherever Thoreau looked, whether at people or at the things people believed in, he found the deep and simple truths ignored and the surfaces of things celebrated. The rush to search for gold quite amazed him. "Don't travel to California to find gold," he wrote. "Look for it within yourself." When someone praised Harvard College for teaching "all the branches of knowledge," Thoreau simply answered: "Yes, all the *branches*—but none of the *roots*."

New clothes were not very important to him either. "Sell your clothes and keep your thoughts," he liked to say. But Thoreau had another reason for liking old clothes, too. He said that it takes time for clothes to really fit a person's body. That's another reason he felt sorry for many well-to-do people: they threw their clothes away, he said, before they got comfortable!

You might think that Thoreau, having found peace at Walden, would have stayed there forever. But he left his Walden house after about two years. He explains that even here—where he was freer than he ever had been—a kind of sameness slowly set in, making what he first called "an experiment" seem too routine. "I had other lives to live and could not spare any more time for that one," he later wrote.

Fortunately, he left a record of "that one" life—in his most famous book, *Walden*. Written over several years, the book tells why Thoreau went to Walden, what he did there, and what he believed life's purposes to be.

Walden is not a long book. But it is filled with wonderful sentences that grab at your mind and stay in your ear. With complete ease, Thoreau's best writing moves from luminous description to hard, kernel-like sayings to a kind of word play that is both serious and full of fun. Here are some examples:

> *The bluebird carries the sky on its back.*
> *The rich crackle of burning leaves was like mustard to my ear.*
> *Time is but the stream I go a-fishing in.*
> *The ice on the pond "whooped" in the night, as if it were restless in bed and wanted to turn over.*
> *We know but a few men, a great many coats and breeches.*
> *We should come home from adventures every day.*

There is one mysterious passage in *Walden*. Thoreau writes that he once lost "a hound, a bay horse, and a turtle dove," and that he is still searching for them as the years go by. Readers have long wondered what he meant by this. Some think he is talking about a girl he loved when he was a young man. Others say he is talking about finding a perfect friend. Someone once asked Thoreau himself what he meant by saying he had lost these things. But he only looked the questioner in the eye and asked back: "Haven't you?"

Despite the emphasis in *Walden* on solitude, Thoreau was always interested in people and the wider world. He liked music, dancing, and ice skating. And he had many friends, including some very well-known people. A number of writers and thinkers lived in Concord at this time, and Thoreau knew them all. They included the writers Margaret Fuller and Bronson Alcott (Louisa May's father), the novelist Nathaniel Hawthorne, and the philosopher Ralph Waldo Emerson, who first influenced Thoreau and later became his friend. Thoreau thought and wrote about friendship all his life. "Friends," he once said, "are kind to each other's dreams."

Not that Thoreau wasn't sometimes argumentative and hard to get along with! One acquaintance summed up this side of his personality by saying: "I would as soon take Henry's arm as I would the branch of an elm tree."

But Thoreau could also make fun of himself. Referring to his daily walks, he jokingly gave himself the job title of "inspector of snowstorms and rainstorms." (He later became, in fact, an excellent surveyor.) And when boxloads of his first book—which he had paid to have published—did not sell and were returned to him, he jested to a friend: "I now have a library of 900 books—700 of which I have written myself."

From the start, Thoreau had looked critically at the lives of his neighbors. They were—it seemed to him—far more interested in "making a living" than in "living." But as he grew older, he found himself critical of the government of his country, too.

Once, while still living at Walden, Thoreau was even jailed briefly for refusing to pay a tax. At the time, the United States was waging what Thoreau felt was an unjust war against Mexico. This fact, along with his opposition to slavery—which was still practiced then—led to his taking an unusual stand: he refused to support the government with his tax money. There is a story that Emerson visited Thoreau while the latter was in jail. "What are you doing in there, Henry?" the philosopher is supposed to have asked. To which Thoreau is supposed to have replied: "What are *you* doing out *there?*" Indeed, he later argued, in a famous essay called *Civil Disobedience*, that in a time of injustice, "The true place for a just man is . . . a prison."

But Thoreau was not destined to live for many more years. When he was in his early forties, his health began to fail. Hoping to regain it, he took his last trip away from Concord—this time to Michigan and Minnesota. But it was no use. He returned home a dying man.

Even when he was sick, however, he was cheerful and enjoyed having visitors. People especially remember one thing he said in his last days. When a visitor wondered if he had made his peace with God, Thoreau answered in a whisper: "I don't believe that we have ever quarreled."

While he could still move about, he took one final walk to Walden. Standing for the last time by the quiet water he loved, he may have remembered something he had written years before: "The lake is always young; it has not even one wrinkle for all its ripples."

Finally, on May 6, 1862, Thoreau died.

But that was far from the end of his story. Perhaps the strangest thing about this simple life—so little known to the world of that time—is how it has grown larger since death. It is as if a small seed, quietly and carefully planted, took root and slowly grew into a great tree, towering above the woods. National leaders, such as Mahatma Gandhi in India and Martin Luther King, Jr., have been inspired by Thoreau's ideas. And famous writers have learned from his clear, clean style.

It may be, however, that thousands of unknown readers owe him most of all. Life has changed in many ways since Thoreau's time. Cars, planes, and computers are just some of the new things that have come into the world. But in other ways the world has changed very little. Many people are still unhappy. And many wonder how best to live their lives. "Read not the Times," Thoreau reminds them, "read the Eternities." Which is why people still read a book called *Walden*. And why they still remember a man named Henry David Thoreau.

Some Important Dates in the Life of Thoreau

1817—Thoreau is born on July 12 in Concord, Massachusetts.

1837—Thoreau graduates from Harvard College.

1845—Thoreau moves into his Walden house on July 4.

1849—Thoreau publishes his first book, *A Week on the Concord and Merrimack Rivers;* in the same year he also publishes his most famous short essay, *Civil Disobedience.*

1854—Thoreau publishes his most famous book, *Walden.*

1862—Thoreau dies on May 6 in Concord.

Bibliography

Canby, Henry Seidel. *Thoreau*. Boston: Houghton Mifflin Company, 1939.

Emerson, Ralph Waldo. "Thoreau," in *The Portable Emerson*, ed. Mark Van Doren. New York: The Viking Press, 1946.

Harding, Walter. *The Days of Henry Thoreau*. Princeton, NJ: Princeton University Press, 1983.

Harding, Walter. *A Thoreau Handbook*. New York: New York University Press, 1959.

Krutch, Joseph Wood. *Henry David Thoreau*. New York: William Sloane Associates, 1948.

Lebeaux, Richard. *Young Man Thoreau*. Amherst, MA: University of Massachusetts Press, 1977.

Roach, Marilynne K. *Down to Earth at Walden*. Boston: Houghton Mifflin Company, 1980.

Thoreau, Henry David. *Walden and Other Writings*. ed. Brooks Atkinson. New York: Random House, 1950.

Thoreau, Henry David. *The Wisdom of Thoreau*. New York: Pyramid Publications, Inc. 1968.